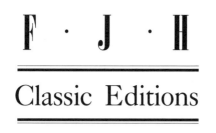

F · J · H

Classic Editions

H 1020

STEPHEN HELLER

Selected Etudes

OPP. 45, 46, AND 47

EDITED BY
EDWIN McLEAN

Production: Frank J. Hackinson
Production Coordinators: Peggy Gallagher and Philip Groeber
Engraving: Tempo Music Press
Printer: Tempo Music Press

ISBN-13: 978-1-61928-226-1

BIOGRAPHY

Stephen Heller (1813-1888)
Image by Alfred Lemoine

Stephen Heller was born in Pest (now Budapest), Hungary. He studied piano with Anton Halm in Vienna. While in Vienna he met Robert Schumann, who was an early champion of his music.

In 1838, Heller moved to Paris, where he remained for the rest of his life. There he was a successful performer, teacher, and music critic. Among his friends were Chopin, Berlioz, and Liszt.

Most of Heller's compositional works are for piano. Among his best known works are three sets of etudes, all written in 1844: Op. 45, *25 Études à l'art de phraser* (25 Etudes on the Art of Phrasing); Op. 46, *30 Études progressives* (30 Progressive Etudes); and Op. 47, *25 Études pour former au sentiment du rhythme et à l'expression* (25 Etudes to develop a feeling of rhythm and expression).

Heller had a relatively long career as a composer. His later works can be viewed as transitional to the Impressionist era—they are coloristic and harmonically adventurous.

TABLE OF CONTENTS

Selected Etudes
No.   **Page**

I wanted to give young students and amateurs the opportunity to execute a piece with expression, grace, elegance, and energy according to the special character of the composition.

Stephen Heller
Preface to Op. 47

About the Edition

We often define an etude as an excercise which focuses on a particular aspect of technique. However, Heller apparently did not see that as the primary purpose of his etudes; instead he thought of the etude as a character piece. It is an artistic miniature designed to develop overall musicianship, focusing on "expression, grace, and elegance." In this respect, his etudes differ from those of Chopin, whose etudes—while masterworks of the highest order—concentrated on a single technical challenge. For Heller, technique was always in service of expression.

For this edition, I have selected from Opp. 45, 46, and 47 some of the easier pieces, that is, easier technically if not musically—all of them require artistry and musicianship. The primary sources for this edition are: Op. 45, Milan/F. Lucca (1845); Op. 46, various 19th century editions such as Schuberth, C. F. Peters, and Liebling; and Op. 47, Berlin/ Schlesinger (1849). These early editions are very specific with respect to phrasing, dynamics, and articulation, so it has not been necessary to add them. For a few etudes that have no pedal markings, occasional pedaling has been added. I have also modernized some of the notation. Two of the etudes are not in sequential order; this was done to create optimal page turns for the performer.

Edwin McLean

Edwin McLean

Op. 45, No. 1
("The Brook")

Stephen Heller

Allegretto; sempre legato e eguale (♩ = ca. 120)

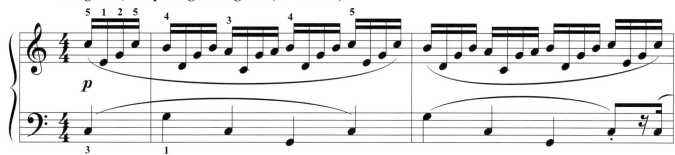

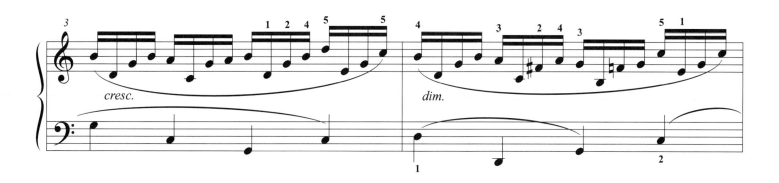

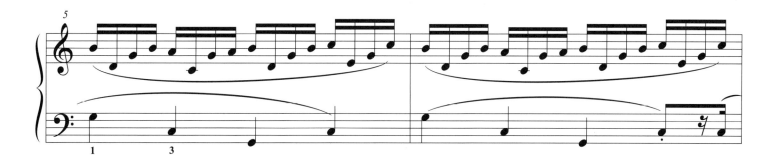

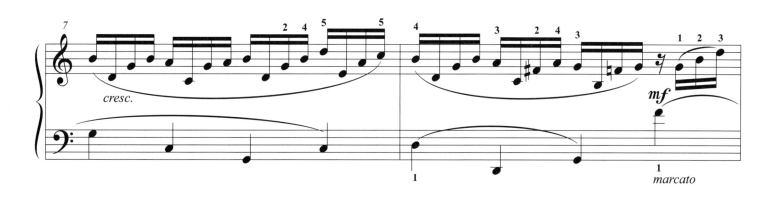

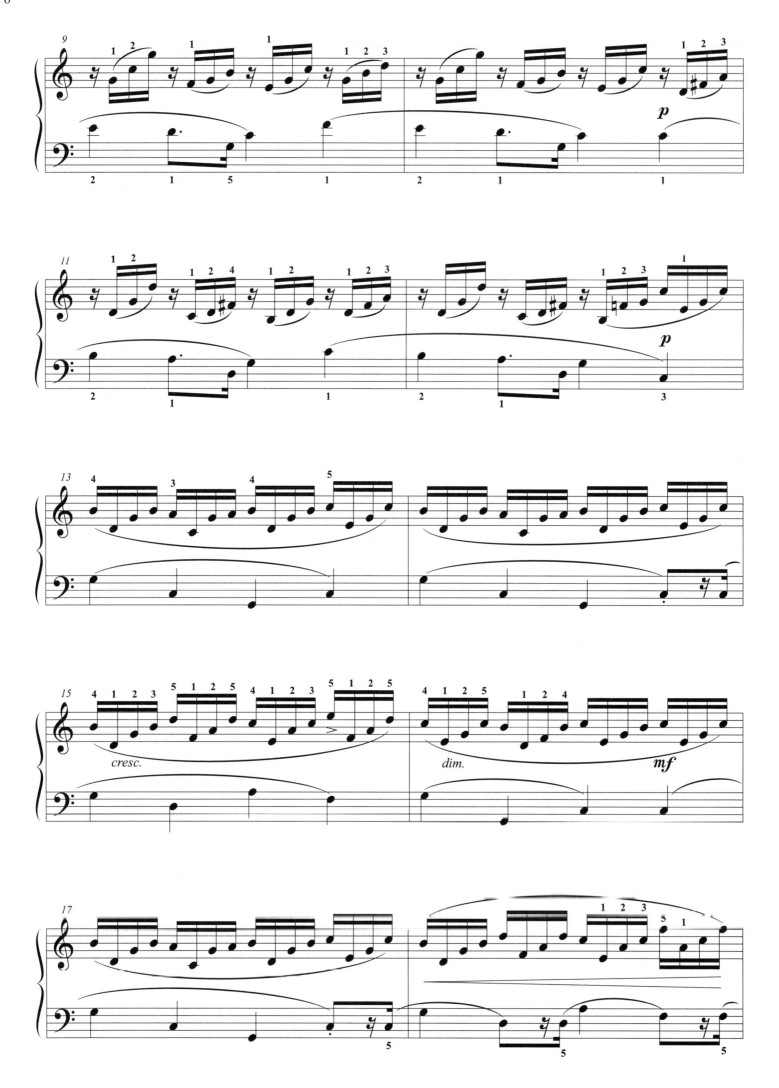

Op. 45, No. 2
("L'Avalanche")

Op. 45, No. 4

("Sorrow and Joy")

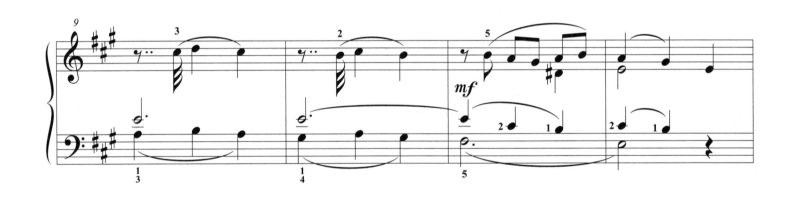

14

Op. 45, No. 5
("Song of May")

Allegretto comodo (♩ = ca. 104)

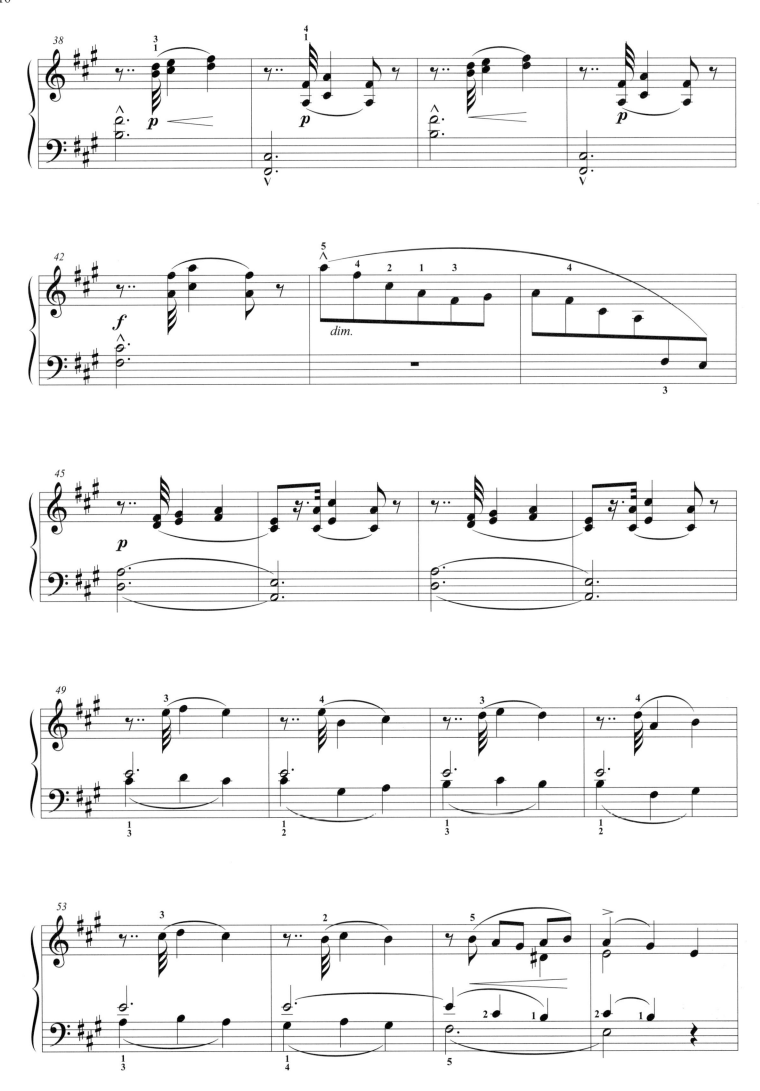

Op. 45, No.18

("Impatience")

Vivo

Op. 45, No.16
("Il Penseroso")

Op. 46, No. 6

Allegretto grazioso (♩ = ca. 120)

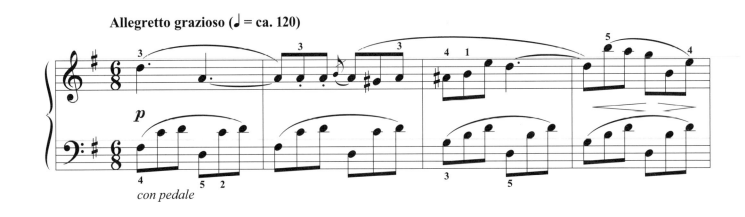

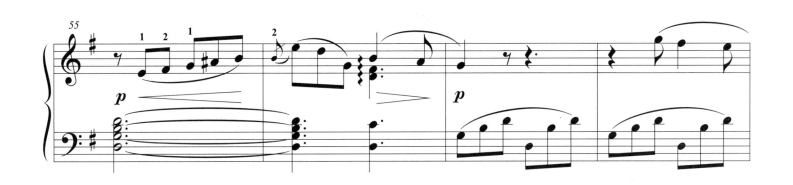

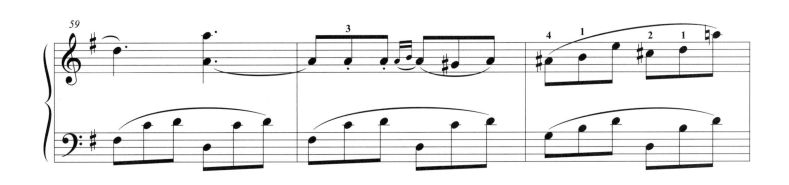

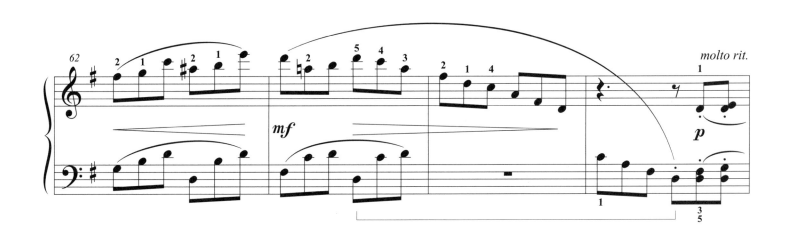

Op. 46, No. 7

Op. 47, No. 1

Op. 47, No. 2

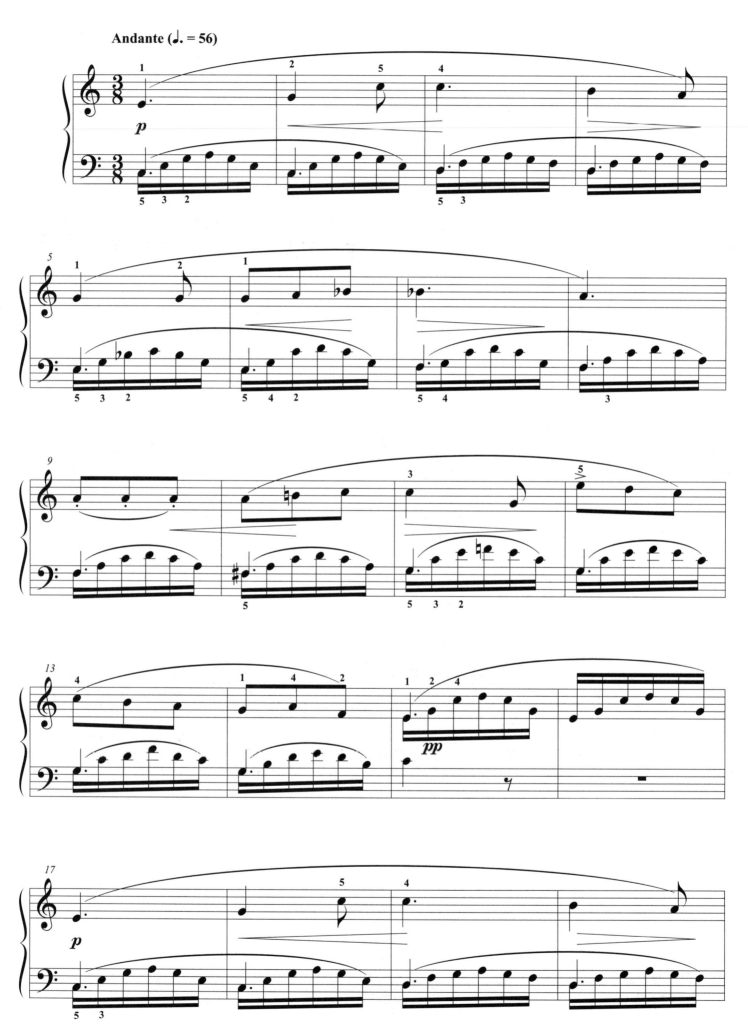

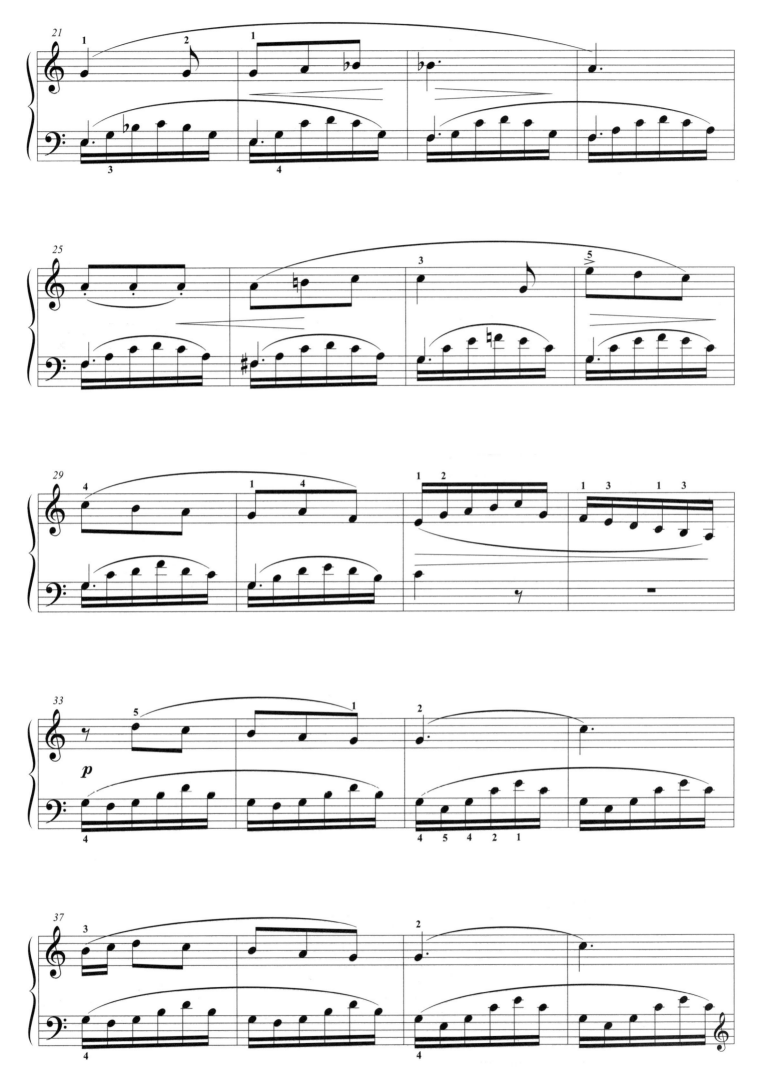

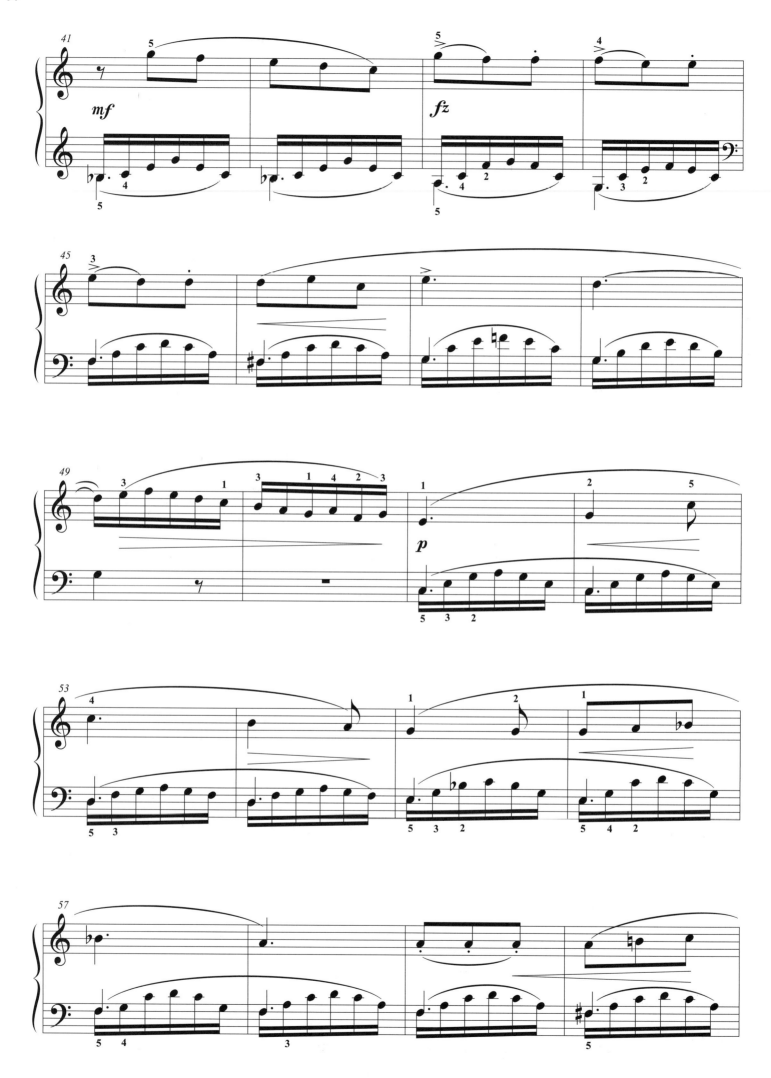

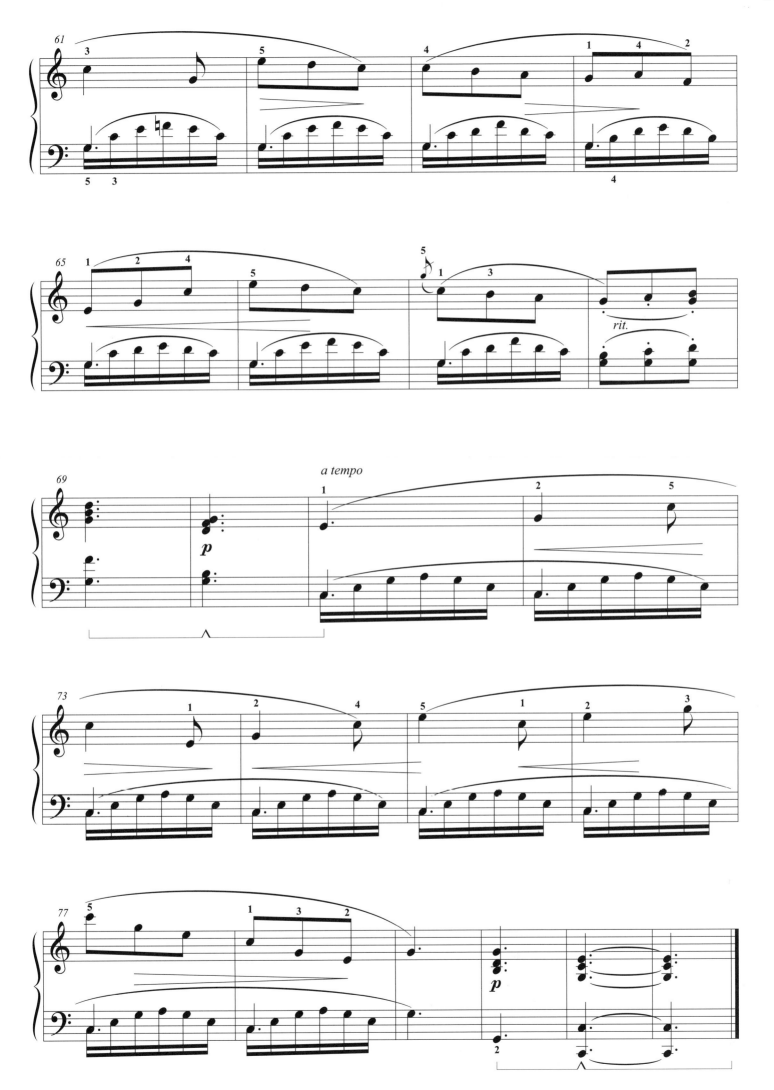

Op. 47, No. 3

Allegretto (♩. = 100)

Op. 47, No. 5

Allegretto poco agitato (♩ = 126)

Op. 47, No. 15

Adagio (♩ = 72)

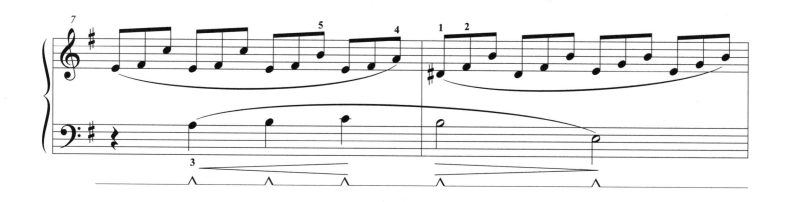

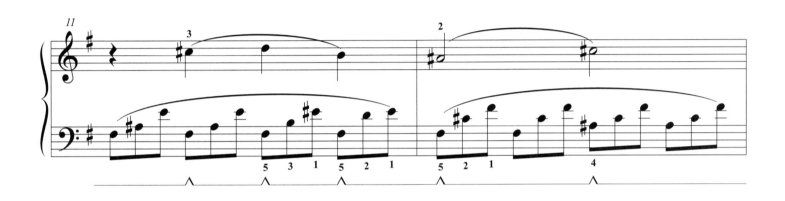

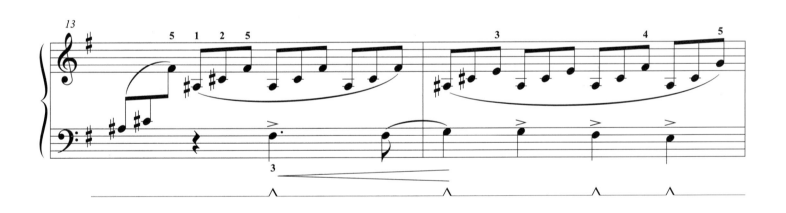

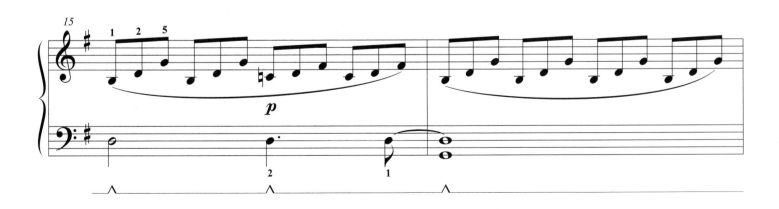

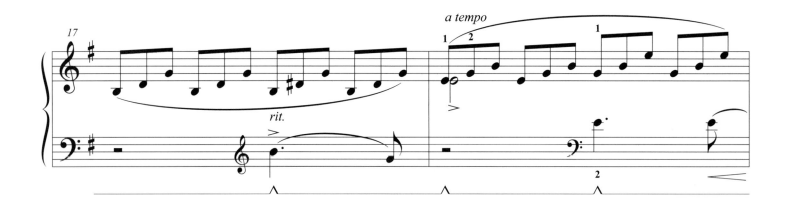

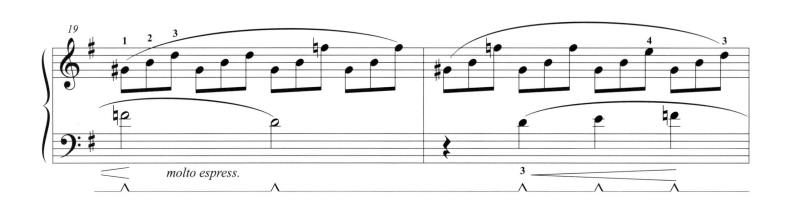

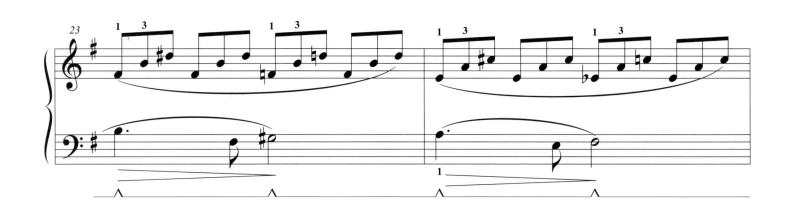

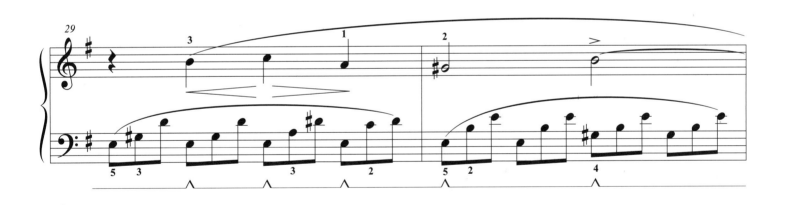

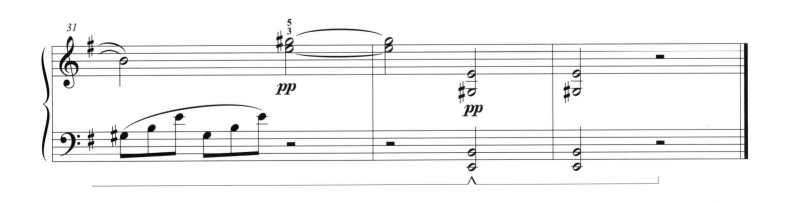

Op. 47, No. 8

Vivace assai (♩. = ca. 76)

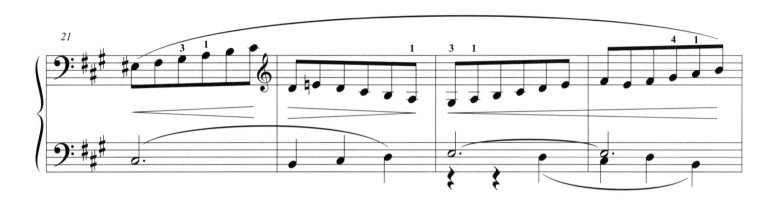

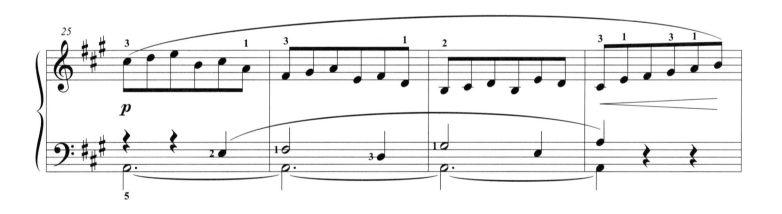

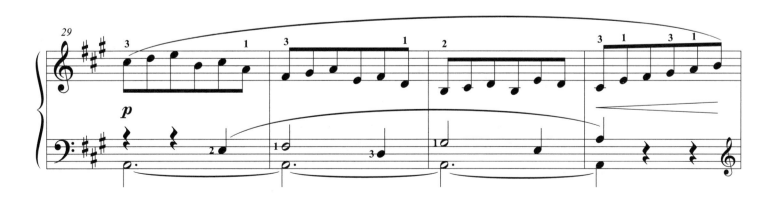

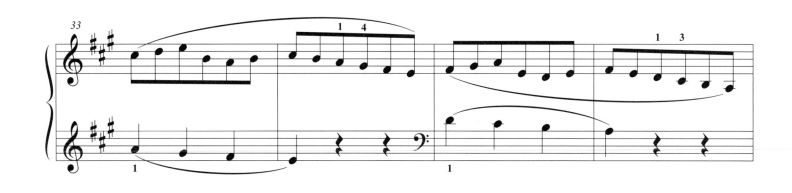

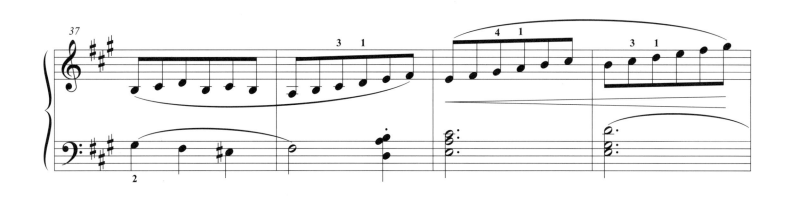

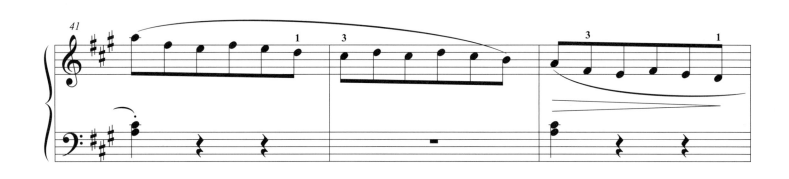

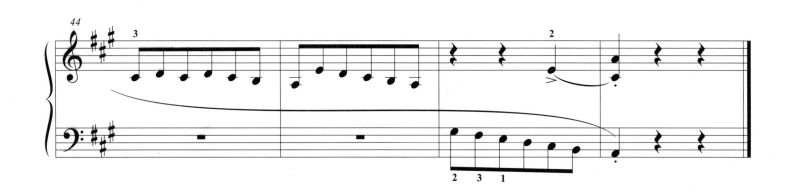